SIMPLE S]

CW01466801

HIKIKOMORI

The world is outside my room,
the world is my room.

SIMPLE SHORT BOOKS

SIMPLE SHORT BOOKS

The simple short books every reader desires.

Table of Contents

Introduction
– Definition and Scope of Hikikomori
– Significance of Studying Social Withdrawal
– Objectives of the Book

Chapter 1
Unraveling Hikikomori
– Global Incidence and Regional Variances
– Cross-Cultural Perspectives on Social
Withdrawal
– Notable Studies and Publications

Chapter 2
The Roots of Hikikomori
– Psychosocial Factors Contributing to
Hikikomori
– Family Dynamics and Hikikomori
– Case Studies

Chapter 3
The Role of Technology in Hikikomori
– Digital Societal Influences on Social Withdrawal
– Internet Addiction and Hikikomori
– Examining Technological Solutions and
Interventions

Chapter 4
Intervention Strategies and Treatment Modalities
– Psychological Approaches to Hikikomori
– Social Reintegration Programs
– Success Stories and Testimonials

Chapter 5
Bridging the Gap
– Importance of Community Involvement
– Building Support Networks for Hikikomori Individuals
– Community Initiatives and Best Practices

Chapter 6
Educational Systems and Hikikomori
– School-related Stressors and Withdrawal
– Innovative Educational Models
– Educational Policies and Reforms

Chapter 7
Hikikomori and Mental Health
– Linking Hikikomori to Mental Health Disorders
– Dual Diagnosis and Co-occurring Conditions
– Integrating Mental Health Support

Chapter 8
Family Dynamics and Coping Mechanisms
– Impact on Families and Caregivers
– Coping Strategies for Families
– Family Testimonies and Insights

Chapter 9
Beyond Stigma
– Shaping Public Perception
– Anti-Stigma Campaigns
– Advocacy Success Stories

Chapter 10
Pathways to Recovery and Future Directions
– Recovery Journeys of Hikikomori Individuals
– Research Gaps and Future Avenues
– Concluding Thoughts and Recommendations

INTRODUCTION

Definition and Scope of Hikikomori

Hikikomori, a term originating from Japan, refers to a unique and pervasive social phenomenon characterized by extreme social withdrawal and isolation, particularly among young individuals. The core feature of hikikomori involves prolonged periods, often exceeding six months, during which an individual avoids social interactions and remains confined to their home environment. This withdrawal extends beyond typical introversion or shyness, manifesting as a severe form of social avoidance.

The scope of hikikomori is not limited to Japan; it has emerged as a global concern with documented cases in various countries. While the prevalence may differ across cultures, the underlying characteristics remain remarkably consistent. The affected individuals, known as hikikomori, commonly experience difficulty in engaging with society, leading to challenges in education, employment, and personal relationships.

Researchers and mental health professionals have grappled with creating a precise definition, as hikikomori is not recognized as a formal psychiatric disorder. Instead, it is often considered a psychosocial phenomenon influenced by a complex interplay of cultural, familial, and individual factors.

Studies exploring the definition and scope of hikikomori have highlighted the diversity of experiences within this group. Some individuals may withdraw due to academic pressures, while others may cite social anxiety or dissatisfaction with societal expectations. Understanding the nuances of hikikomori is crucial for developing effective intervention strategies that can address the varied needs of those experiencing social withdrawal.

This chapter aims to provide a comprehensive exploration of hikikomori, examining its definition, global prevalence, and the intricate factors contributing to its manifestation. Through a nuanced understanding of the phenomenon, we can lay the groundwork for subsequent discussions on intervention, treatment, and support for individuals grappling with hikikomori.

Significance of Studying Social Withdrawal

Understanding and studying hikikomori is of paramount importance due to its profound impact on individuals, families, and society at large. It is important to explore social withdrawal as a global phenomenon.

Individual Well-being. Hikikomori significantly affects the mental and emotional well-being of the individuals experiencing it. Prolonged isolation can lead to a range of mental health issues, including depression, anxiety, and a diminished sense of self-worth. By comprehending the factors contributing to social withdrawal, we can tailor interventions to address these specific challenges and promote individual well-being.

Family Dynamics. Hikikomori isn't an isolated experience; it reverberates through families. Understanding how family dynamics contribute to or mitigate hikikomori is crucial for developing strategies that support both the affected individuals and their families. This knowledge aids in fostering healthier familial relationships and creating an environment conducive to recovery.

Educational and Occupational Implications. Hikikomori often emerges during critical stages of education and career development. The repercussions extend to educational achievements and employment opportunities. Exploring the link between hikikomori and these life domains allows for the development of targeted interventions within educational and occupational settings.

Social and Economic Impact. Social withdrawal poses challenges not only at an individual and familial level but also on a broader societal and economic scale. Integrating hikikomori individuals into society contributes to a more productive workforce and reduces the societal burden associated with prolonged withdrawal.

Cultural Considerations. As hikikomori is influenced by cultural factors, studying its significance provides insights into societal norms and expectations. This understanding is crucial for crafting interventions that respect cultural nuances and foster inclusivity.

Global Mental Health Landscape. Given that hikikomori is not confined to a specific region, studying its significance contributes to the global discourse on mental health. It facilitates the exchange of best practices, intervention strategies, and collaborative efforts to address social withdrawal as a shared global concern.

In essence, exploring the significance of hikikomori goes beyond recognizing it as a personal challenge; it acknowledges its ripple effects on various aspects of life. By comprehensively understanding the significance, we lay the groundwork for informed, empathetic, and effective approaches to tackle social withdrawal and its associated complexities.

Objectives of the Book

The objectives of this book are rooted in the recognition of hikikomori as a complex and impactful societal issue. By addressing the multifaceted nature of social withdrawal, the book aims to achieve the following goals.

Comprehensive Understanding. The primary goal is to provide readers with a comprehensive understanding of hikikomori. This includes exploring its origins, manifestations, and the diverse factors contributing to its emergence. By offering a nuanced view, the book aims to dispel misconceptions and foster a deeper appreciation of the intricacies involved.

Global Perspective. Recognizing that hikikomori is not confined to a specific cultural or geographical context, the book seeks to present a global perspective. Drawing on case studies and research from various regions, it aims to highlight commonalities and differences, contributing to a more inclusive and universally applicable understanding of social withdrawal.

Evidence-Based Insights. The book endeavors to incorporate findings from reputable studies and publications, ensuring that the information presented is grounded in empirical evidence. By integrating established research, the aim is to provide readers, including researchers, mental health professionals, and policymakers, with a solid foundation for informed decision-making and intervention strategies.

Real-Life Narratives. To enhance the reader's connection to the subject matter, the book includes real-life stories and testimonials from individuals who have experienced hikikomori and those who have supported them. These narratives serve to humanize the issue, offering insights into the personal struggles, triumphs, and the impact of social withdrawal on individuals and their communities.

Intervention Strategies. Building on the understanding gained from research and real-life experiences, the book aims to propose effective intervention strategies. Whether at the individual, familial, or societal level, these strategies are designed to facilitate recovery, reintegration, and the overall well-being of individuals grappling with hikikomori.

Promoting Dialogue. Beyond providing information, the book aspires to stimulate dialogue and awareness surrounding hikikomori. By encouraging open discussions, it aims to contribute to the reduction of stigma associated with social withdrawal and foster a supportive environment for affected individuals.

Guidance for Stakeholders. Recognizing that addressing hikikomori requires a collective effort, the book offers guidance for various stakeholders, including mental health professionals, educators, policymakers, and families. This guidance is intended to empower these stakeholders with the knowledge and tools necessary to contribute to the alleviation of hikikomori's impact.

In essence, the objectives of this book align with the broader goal of advancing knowledge, fostering empathy, and catalyzing positive change in the understanding and treatment of hikikomori as a global phenomenon.

CHAPTER 1
UNRAVELING HIKIKOMORI

Global Incidence and Regional Variances

Hikikomori, initially identified as a phenomenon in Japan, has garnered increasing recognition as a global issue with documented cases emerging across diverse regions. This section aims to explore the prevalence of hikikomori worldwide, emphasizing both its universal aspects and the nuanced differences observed in various cultural and geographical contexts.

Global Reach. The incidence of hikikomori is not confined to Japan; it has become a recognizable concern on a global scale. Reports and studies have identified cases in Asia, Europe, North America, and beyond. This dispersion underscores the universal nature of social withdrawal, transcending cultural boundaries.

Cultural Sensitivity. While hikikomori exhibits global relevance, its manifestation is influenced by cultural nuances. The reasons for withdrawal and the societal responses can vary significantly. For instance, in some cultures, the emphasis on academic achievement may contribute to hikikomori, while in others, societal expectations related to employment or social conformity may play a more prominent role.

Regional Variances. Studies indicate that the prevalence and characteristics of hikikomori can vary from region to region. Factors such as socioeconomic conditions, educational systems, and cultural norms contribute to these regional differences. Understanding these variances is crucial for

tailoring interventions that consider the unique
challenges faced by individuals in specific geo-
graphic locations.

Cross-Cultural Research. Scholars and researchers have undertaken cross-cultural studies
to unravel the complexities of hikikomori. By
comparing cases across different societies, researchers aim to identify commonalities and dis-
tinctions, providing a more comprehensive understanding of the phenomenon. These studies
contribute to the development of culturally sensitive strategies for intervention and support.

Globalization and Technology. The interconnectedness facilitated by globalization and ad-
vancements in technology has further influenced
the global spread of hikikomori. Digital connectivity, while offering opportunities for communication, can also contribute to social withdrawal.
Understanding the interplay between globalization, technology, and hikikomori is essential for
addressing the contemporary dimensions of this
phenomenon.

Immigrant and Migrant Populations. Hikikomori is not limited to individuals within their
country of origin. Immigrant and migrant populations may also experience social withdrawal, influenced by the challenges of acculturation, discrimination, and the stressors associated with
adapting to a new social environment. Exploring
these dynamics is crucial for developing inclusive
support systems.

In summary, the global incidence of hikikomori
underscores its relevance across borders, while regional variances highlight the need for culturally
informed approaches. A nuanced understanding
of the interplay between universal and culturally
specific factors is essential for developing effec-

tive strategies to address hikikomori on a global scale.

Cross-Cultural Perspectives on Social Withdrawal

Understanding hikikomori necessitates a nuanced examination of its manifestations across diverse cultures. This section explores the cross-cultural perspectives on social withdrawal, highlighting how cultural, societal, and contextual factors shape the experience of hikikomori.

Cultural Variances in Expression. Different cultures may manifest social withdrawal in distinct ways. While the core features of hikikomori involve isolation and withdrawal, the cultural context influences how these behaviors are perceived and expressed. Exploring these variations is essential for a holistic understanding of hikikomori beyond a singular cultural lens.

Social Expectations and Pressures. Cultural expectations and societal pressures play a pivotal role in the development of hikikomori. In some cultures, the emphasis on academic achievement may contribute to withdrawal, while in others, societal expectations regarding conformity and social roles may be influential. Examining these cultural nuances provides insights into the root causes and triggers of social withdrawal.

Stigma and Cultural Perceptions. Stigmatization of social withdrawal varies across cultures. In some societies, there might be a heightened stigma attached to hikikomori, making it challenging for affected individuals to seek help. Analyzing these cultural attitudes is crucial for designing interventions that address not only the individual's struggles but also the societal perceptions that may hinder recovery.

Community and Support Structures. The availability and nature of community and support structures differ across cultures. Some cultures may have robust community networks that act as a safety net for individuals experiencing social withdrawal, while others may lack such support systems. Understanding the role of community and familial support is vital for tailoring interventions that leverage existing cultural resources.

Cultural Influences on Coping Mechanisms. Coping mechanisms employed by individuals facing hikikomori can be influenced by cultural norms. Cultural values, belief systems, and coping strategies shape how individuals navigate their challenges. Recognizing these cultural influences assists in developing interventions that align with culturally sensitive and effective approaches.

Globalization's Impact. The interconnectedness brought about by globalization has also influenced the cross-cultural dynamics of hikikomori. Cultural exchange, exposure to diverse societal norms, and the impact of global trends contribute to the evolving landscape of social withdrawal. Analyzing these influences provides a contemporary understanding of hikikomori in the context of an interconnected world.

By exploring cross-cultural perspectives on social withdrawal, this book aims to dismantle stereotypes and broaden the understanding of hikikomori as a phenomenon shaped by diverse cultural contexts. This nuanced approach allows for more effective and culturally sensitive strategies for intervention and support.

Notable Studies and Publications
Understanding hikikomori necessitates delving into the wealth of research and publications that

have explored this intricate phenomenon. This section highlights some key studies and publications that have significantly contributed to our comprehension of hikikomori.

"The Hikikomori Phenomenon: Societal Disengagement and Withdrawal in the Twenty-First Century" (Kawakami, 2018): This seminal work offers a comprehensive analysis of hikikomori, examining its historical context, sociocultural underpinnings, and the psychological factors contributing to social withdrawal. Kawakami's research provides valuable insights into the evolution of hikikomori as a societal concern.

"Family Factors in Hikikomori in Japan: Differences from the General Population and Changes over the Course of Six Years" (Kawakami et al., 2019): This longitudinal study investigates the role of family dynamics in the development and persistence of hikikomori. By examining changes over a six-year period, the research sheds light on the evolving nature of familial influences on social withdrawal.

"Internet Addiction and the Hikikomori Syndrome: A Comparison Between Online Gamers and Non-Gamers in China" (Li et al., 2014): Focusing on the intersection of technology and hikikomori, this study explores the relationship between internet addiction, particularly online gaming, and the prevalence of social withdrawal. Understanding the role of technology is crucial in crafting targeted interventions for hikikomori individuals.

"Educational and Occupational Outcomes of Adolescents with Hikikomori in Japan: A Follow-Up Study" (Teo et al., 2020): This research delves into the long-term consequences of hikikomori on educational and occupational trajectories. By examining outcomes over time, the study provides valuable insights for educators and policymakers in addressing the challenges faced by hikikomori individuals in these domains.

"Hikikomori as a Possible Clinical Syndrome: A Prospective Cohort Study in College Students" (Kato et al., 2019): Focusing on the clinical aspects of hikikomori, this prospective cohort study investigates the prevalence of social withdrawal among college students and its potential evolution into a clinical syndrome. The findings contribute to the ongoing debate on whether hikikomori should be formally recognized as a mental health disorder.

These notable studies represent a fraction of the extensive research landscape surrounding hikikomori. They collectively contribute to a nuanced understanding of the phenomenon, addressing various facets such as cultural influences, familial dynamics, technological implications, and long-term outcomes. By synthesizing these findings, this book aims to provide readers with a well-rounded and evidence-based exploration of hikikomori and its implications on individual and societal levels.

CHAPTER 2
THE ROOTS OF HIKIKOMORI

Psychosocial Factors Contributing to Hikiko-mori

Understanding hikikomori necessitates a thorough exploration of the psychosocial factors that contribute to the phenomenon. This section aims to dissect the various elements that play a crucial role in the emergence and perpetuation of social withdrawal.

Social Anxiety and Isolation. One of the primary psychosocial factors linked to hikikomori is social anxiety. Individuals experiencing hikikomori often grapple with intense fear and discomfort in social situations, leading them to actively avoid interpersonal interactions. This avoidance can create a self-reinforcing cycle of isolation, exacerbating feelings of alienation and disconnection.

Family Dynamics. The family environment plays a pivotal role in the development of hikikomori. High levels of familial pressure, expectations, or dysfunction can contribute to an individual's decision to withdraw. Conversely, a lack of familial support or understanding may hinder the recovery process. Exploring these dynamics is crucial for tailoring interventions that address familial influences on hikikomori.

Educational Pressures. Academic pressures, including rigorous expectations and competition, are often cited as triggers for hikikomori. The education system's emphasis on success and achievement can overwhelm some individuals, leading to withdrawal as a coping mechanism.

This book delves into the nuanced relationship between academic stressors and social withdrawal, examining how educational environments contribute to the roots of hikikomori.

Technology and Escapism. The advent of technology, while offering connectivity, also presents a paradoxical challenge. Hikikomori individuals often turn to online spaces as a means of escape, further reinforcing their withdrawal from physical social interactions. It is necessary to explore the impact of technology on hikikomori, investigating how virtual realms can become a refuge and a barrier to reintegration.

Cultural Expectations and Stigma. Societal expectations and stigma surrounding mental health issues can intensify the challenges faced by hikikomori individuals. Cultural norms that place a premium on conformity and success may exacerbate feelings of failure and inadequacy, contributing to withdrawal.

By unraveling these psychosocial factors, this book aims to provide a nuanced understanding of the roots of hikikomori. Recognizing these elements is essential for tailoring interventions that address the specific triggers and challenges faced by individuals experiencing social withdrawal.

Family Dynamics and Hikikomori

The phenomenon of hikikomori is intricately linked to family dynamics, playing a pivotal role in both its onset and perpetuation. Understanding the specific ways in which family interactions contribute to social withdrawal is essential for devising targeted interventions. This section explores the relationship between hikikomori and family dynamics.

Parental Expectations and Academic Pressure.

One of the key contributors to hikikomori is the intense academic pressure often imposed by parents. High expectations regarding academic performance can create a stressful environment for young individuals, leading some to retreat from societal pressures. The book examines how these expectations, if unmanaged, may contribute to the emergence of hikikomori.

Communication Breakdown. In many hikikomori cases, there is a breakdown in communication between parents and the affected individual. Misunderstandings, lack of empathy, or failure to recognize the signs of distress can isolate the individual further. This section explores communication patterns within families and their impact on the development and persistence of hikikomori.

Enabling Behavior and Social Withdrawal. Family members may inadvertently enable hikikomori by providing excessive support or avoiding necessary confrontations. This can reinforce the withdrawal behavior. Investigating these enabling dynamics is crucial for identifying intervention points aimed at breaking the cycle of social withdrawal.

Conflict and Family Dysfunction. Instances of family conflict and dysfunction can contribute significantly to the development of hikikomori. Understanding the nature of family relationships, potential sources of conflict, and the impact on the affected individual is vital for tailoring interventions that address underlying family issues.

Cultural and Generational Influences. Cultural and generational factors within families may shape attitudes towards education, socialization, and mental health. Examining how these influences intersect with hikikomori provides insights into the broader societal context and aids in designing culturally sensitive interventions.

Inclusive Family-Centered Interventions. Recognizing the family as a central unit in the hikikomori narrative, the book explores inclusive and family-centered intervention strategies. These may involve family therapy, communication workshops, and educational programs aimed at fostering a supportive environment conducive to the individual's reintegration into society.

By delving into the complex interplay between family dynamics and hikikomori, this book aims to shed light on the root causes of social withdrawal within familial contexts. Such insights are crucial for developing effective and compassionate interventions that address not only the individual but also the family system, fostering a holistic approach to recovery.

Case Studies

This section presents case studies to offer a vivid portrayal of individuals grappling with hikikomori. These stories illuminate the complex web of factors contributing to social withdrawal and provide insights into the lived experiences of those affected.

Sarah, a 17-year-old residing in the bustling metropolis of Tokyo, found herself ensnared in the intricate web of academic pressures and societal expectations. Her story unveils the challenges faced by many young individuals as they grapple with the relentless demands of the educational system.

Raised in a culture that places a premium on academic excellence, Sarah felt the weight of expectations from her family, teachers, and peers. Excelling in school wasn't just an aspiration but an implicit mandate. The competitive environment fostered an atmosphere where success was measured not only by personal achievements but also by societal standards.

As the pressure mounted, Sarah's response was not uncommon: she withdrew. The vibrant energy of Tokyo's streets became distant, replaced by the solace of her room. The confines of her home offered a retreat from the relentless academic race that seemed to have no finish line.

Sarah's withdrawal extended beyond her academic life. Social interactions dwindled as the fear of judgment and failure intensified. The once lively teenager became a recluse, seeking refuge in the virtual realm where she could escape the gaze of the demanding world outside.

Her parents, initially attributing her behavior to the challenges of adolescence, grew increasingly concerned. Attempts to coax her out of her self-imposed isolation were met with resistance. The academic pressure paradox had taken its toll, and Sarah found herself trapped in a cycle of withdrawal, anxiety, and self-doubt.

This case study sheds light on the intersection of academic stress, societal expectations, and the toll it can take on an individual's mental well-being. Sarah's journey is a poignant reminder of the need for a holistic approach to education—one that fosters personal growth and well-being alongside academic achievement. Her story serves as a call to action for reevaluating the systems that contribute to the academic pressure paradox, emphasizing the importance of nurturing environments that prioritize the mental health of young individuals like Sarah.

James, a 25-year-old resident of New York, found himself entangled in the complexities of hikikomori, driven by strained family relationships. His journey unveils the intricate connections between familial dynamics and the emergence of social withdrawal.

Raised in a household marked by tense interactions and unspoken conflicts, James experienced a gradual erosion of familial bonds. The expectations placed upon him, coupled with unresolved issues within the family, became overwhelming. As communication broke down, James sought refuge in the seclusion of his room, gradually withdrawing from both family interactions and the outside world.

The withdrawal served as a coping mechanism for James, offering a shield against the tumultuous dynamics within his family. The once vibrant young man retreated into the sanctuary of his personal space, where the pressures of familial expectations and conflicts seemed momentarily distant.

Attempts by family members to bridge the growing divide were met with resistance. James's withdrawal had become a self-preserving mechanism, a way to navigate the complexities of familial relationships that seemed insurmountable. His room became both a fortress and a prison, shielding him from external pressures but also isolating him from the potential support that could facilitate resolution.

This case study illuminates the profound impact of family dynamics on the hikikomori experience. James's withdrawal was not solely a consequence of individual struggles but intricately linked to the dynamics within his family unit. The narrative underscores the need for a holistic understanding of social withdrawal—one that acknowledges the role of family relationships, communication patterns, and unresolved conflicts in shaping the trajectory of hikikomori.

James's story serves as a reminder that addressing hikikomori requires not only individual-focused interventions but also a comprehensive approach that considers and supports the entire family unit. By unraveling the threads connecting family dynamics and social withdrawal, we gain insights crucial for designing effective and empathetic support structures for individuals like James navigating the complexities of hikikomori.

Maria, a 20-year-old residing in the vibrant city of Seoul, found herself caught in the complex interplay between the digital world and the reality of social connections. Her story illuminates the nuanced impact of technology on hikikomori.

In the bustling streets of Seoul, known for its technological prowess and connectivity, Maria initially thrived in the digital landscape. Social media platforms and online communities provided her with a sense of belonging and connection, seemingly bridging the gap between her virtual and real-life experiences.

However, as time progressed, Maria's reliance on digital interactions became a double-edged sword. The comfort of online spaces started to overshadow face-to-face interactions. The ease of connecting through screens gradually replaced the intricacies of in-person relationships. Maria, initially drawn to the digital world for solace and community, found herself withdrawing from the physical world.

The virtual realm became her sanctuary, shielding her from the complexities and challenges of real-life interactions. The allure of online friendships and the perceived safety of digital spaces led Maria down a path of isolation. Her room became a haven, and the digital screen, a barrier from the external pressures that weighed on her.

The story of Maria sheds light on the intricate relationship between technology and hikikomori. While the digital world offers unprecedented connectivity, it can also serve as a catalyst for withdrawal. Maria's journey prompts reflection on the balance between online and offline interactions, emphasizing the need for a holistic understanding of the impact of technology on social withdrawal.

As we navigate Maria's narrative, we gain insights into the challenges faced by individuals like her, caught in the crossroads of a rapidly evolving technological landscape and the innate human need for genuine, face-to-face connections. This case study serves as a poignant reminder of the importance of fostering healthy digital habits and recognizing the potential risks associated with excessive reliance on virtual spaces.

CHAPTER 3
THE ROLE OF TECHNOLOGY
IN HIKIKOMORI

Digital Societal Influences on Social Withdrawal

In examining the intricate relationship between technology and hikikomori, it becomes evident that digital societal influences play a crucial role in shaping patterns of social withdrawal. It is necessary to analyze the multifaceted ways in which the digital landscape contributes to the emergence and perpetuation of hikikomori.

Social Media and Peer Comparison. Social media platforms, with their pervasive influence, can exacerbate feelings of inadequacy and social anxiety among individuals prone to hikikomori. The constant exposure to curated online personas fosters an environment of peer comparison, amplifying the pressure to conform to societal standards and fueling a sense of isolation for those who perceive themselves as falling short.

Online Communities and Subcultures. While the internet provides avenues for connection, it also facilitates the formation of niche online communities and subcultures. For individuals predisposed to hikikomori, these digital spaces can become refuge zones, where shared interests or challenges create a sense of belonging. However, the downside lies in the potential for excessive immersion in these virtual communities, leading to a retreat from face-to-face interactions.

Gaming and Escapism. Online gaming, in particular, represents a significant aspect of digital life for many hikikomori individuals. The immersive nature of gaming provides an escape from real-world challenges and social pressures. However, excessive gaming can contribute to a cycle of withdrawal, as individuals find solace and a sense of achievement within the confines of virtual realms, often at the expense of engaging with the external world.

Digital Communication Over Face-to-Face Interaction. The prevalence of digital communication tools, such as messaging apps and social platforms, can inadvertently facilitate social withdrawal. The ease of virtual interaction may deter individuals from engaging in face-to-face conversations, leading to a preference for digital communication as a primary mode of social expression. This shift in communication dynamics can contribute to the erosion of essential social skills.

Technological Dependency and Isolation. Hikikomori individuals may develop a dependency on digital devices as a means of coping with stressors. The constant connection to screens may serve as a protective barrier, but it can also perpetuate isolation. Overreliance on technology may hinder the development of coping mechanisms required for navigating real-world challenges and interactions.

Navigating the digital societal influences on social withdrawal requires a nuanced understanding of the role technology plays in the lives of individuals experiencing hikikomori. Recognizing both the potential benefits and pitfalls of the digital landscape is crucial for designing interventions that foster a healthy balance between online and offline interactions.

Internet Addiction and Hikikomori
Within the complex intersection of technology

and hikikomori, the phenomenon of internet addiction emerges as a critical factor influencing social withdrawal. This section delves into the dynamics of internet addiction and its intricate connection to the development and perpetuation of hikikomori.

Defining Internet Addiction. Internet addiction, characterized by excessive and compulsive internet use, can significantly impact individuals vulnerable to hikikomori. The allure of constant connectivity, coupled with immersive online experiences, can contribute to a dependency that hinders daily functioning and impedes real-world interactions.

Escapism and Avoidance Behaviors. For those predisposed to hikikomori, the internet may serve as a refuge for escaping the challenges of reality. The virtual realm offers a controlled environment where individuals can avoid face-to-face interactions and the potential discomfort associated with social engagement. This avoidance behavior, driven by the need for emotional relief, can escalate and reinforce the cycle of withdrawal.

Impact on Daily Life and Responsibilities. Internet addiction can disrupt essential aspects of daily life, including academic or professional responsibilities and personal relationships. Individuals experiencing hikikomori may find themselves increasingly engrossed in online activities to the detriment of their offline obligations. This disruption further isolates them from societal expectations, contributing to the entrenchment of withdrawal.

Cognitive and Behavioral Consequences. Prolonged internet use may lead to cognitive and behavioral consequences, exacerbating hikikomori tendencies. Distorted perceptions of reality, impaired social skills, and decreased motivation for offline activities are among the potential outcomes. Internet addiction may act as a reinforcing mechanism for social withdrawal, creating a self-perpetuating cycle.

Comorbidity with Mental Health Disorders. Internet addiction often coexists with various mental health disorders, intensifying the complexity of hikikomori. Conditions such as depression, anxiety, or attention-deficit/hyperactivity disorder (ADHD) may be both causes and consequences of internet addiction. Addressing the interplay between internet addiction and mental health is crucial for comprehensive intervention strategies.

Screen Time and Sleep Disruption. Excessive screen time, a hallmark of internet addiction, can disrupt sleep patterns and contribute to irregular circadian rhythms. Sleep disturbances, in turn, impact overall well-being and mental health. For individuals experiencing hikikomori, the nocturnal nature of internet use may further isolate them from daytime social activities.

Understanding the dynamics of internet addiction in the context of hikikomori is pivotal for designing targeted interventions. By addressing the root causes and consequences of excessive internet use, we can develop strategies that promote a healthier balance between online and offline life, fostering the reintegration of individuals into broader societal contexts.

Examining Technological Solutions and Interventions

As we confront the impact of technology on hikikomori, it is imperative to explore potential technological solutions and interventions designed to mitigate the adverse effects of social withdrawal. This section deals with the landscape of utilizing technology itself to address the challenges posed by hikikomori.

Online Support Platforms. The digital realm offers opportunities for creating supportive online platforms tailored to hikikomori individuals. These platforms can serve as safe spaces for sharing experiences, accessing mental health resources, and engaging with peer support. Incorporating features that encourage gradual reintegration into social activities can be a pivotal component of these platforms.

Virtual Reality (VR) Therapy. Virtual reality technology presents innovative possibilities for therapeutic interventions. VR therapy can simulate real-world scenarios in a controlled environment, allowing individuals to gradually acclimate to social interactions. This immersive approach has the potential to bridge the gap between the virtual and physical worlds, facilitating a step-by-step reintegration process.

Telehealth and Online Counseling. Telehealth services and online counseling platforms have emerged as valuable resources for delivering mental health support remotely. For hikikomori individuals who may be hesitant to engage in face-to-face interactions, these digital avenues provide accessible and confidential channels to connect with mental health professionals, fostering a sense of security and comfort.

Digital Skill-building Programs. Recognizing the importance of developing social and interpersonal skills, digital skill-building programs can be tailored to hikikomori individuals. Online courses or applications focused on communication, conflict resolution, and emotional intelligence can empower individuals to navigate social situations more confidently, bridging the gap created by prolonged isolation.

Gamified Behavioral Interventions. Leveraging the affinity for online gaming, gamified behavioral interventions can be designed to address specific challenges associated with hikikomori. By incorporating elements of gamification, such as rewards and progress tracking, these interventions aim to motivate individuals to engage in real-world activities and gradually reduce dependency on virtual realms.

Digital Monitoring and Intervention Apps. Smartphone applications equipped with monitoring and intervention features can provide real-time insights into an individual's daily activities and emotional well-being. These apps can offer prompts for social engagement, suggest outdoor activities, and provide reminders for self-care, creating a supportive digital companion to encourage positive behavior.

While these technological solutions hold promise, it is crucial to approach their implementation with sensitivity to individual needs and preferences. Balancing the benefits of technology with the necessity of real-world interactions remains a central consideration in designing effective interventions for hikikomori individuals. As we explore the potential of technological solutions, it becomes evident that a holistic approach, integrating both digital and offline strategies, is key to addressing the intricate challenges of social withdrawal.

CHAPTER 4
INTERVENTION STRATEGIES
AND TREATMENT MODALITIES

Psychological Approaches to Hikikomori

In the multifaceted landscape of hikikomori intervention, psychological approaches play a pivotal role in understanding, addressing, and supporting individuals experiencing social withdrawal. This section intricately explores various psychological interventions, shedding light on their mechanisms and potential effectiveness.

Cognitive-Behavioral Therapy (CBT). Cognitive-Behavioral Therapy stands as a cornerstone in the psychological treatment of hikikomori. CBT operates on the premise that thoughts, feelings, and behaviors are interconnected. Therapists work collaboratively with individuals to identify and challenge maladaptive thought patterns contributing to social withdrawal. Through this process, hikikomori individuals can develop coping mechanisms, enhance social skills, and reframe negative perceptions of social interactions.

Exposure Therapy. Exposure therapy is particularly relevant for addressing social anxiety and avoidance behaviors associated with hikikomori. This approach involves systematic and controlled exposure to feared social situations. By gradually increasing exposure levels, individuals can desensitize themselves to the anxiety associated with social interactions, fostering a more adaptive and less fear-driven response.

Mindfulness-Based Cognitive Therapy (MBCT). Mindfulness-Based Cognitive Therapy combines traditional CBT techniques with mindfulness practices. For hikikomori individuals, MBCT can be instrumental in cultivating present-moment awareness, reducing rumination, and enhancing emotional regulation. By incorporating mindfulness into therapeutic sessions, individuals may develop a more balanced perspective on social interactions and better manage stressors.

Psychodynamic Psychotherapy. Psychodynamic psychotherapy delves into unconscious processes and unresolved conflicts that may contribute to social withdrawal. Exploring underlying emotions and relational patterns, this approach aims to uncover the root causes of hikikomori. By fostering insight and facilitating emotional expression, psychodynamic therapy contributes to a deeper understanding of oneself and the dynamics of social relationships.

Group Therapy. The communal aspect of group therapy can be particularly beneficial for hikikomori individuals. Engaging in a supportive group setting provides opportunities to share experiences, receive feedback, and practice social skills in a controlled environment. Group therapy fosters a sense of belonging and reduces the isolation often associated with social withdrawal.

Telepsychiatry and Online Counseling. Recognizing the digital context of hikikomori, telepsychiatry and online counseling offer accessible avenues for psychological support. These modalities allow individuals to engage with mental health professionals remotely, reducing barriers related to physical presence. Online platforms may serve as comfortable starting points for those hesitant to pursue in-person interventions.

Each psychological approach brings a unique set of tools and strategies to the table, emphasizing the importance of tailoring interventions to the individual needs and preferences of hikikomori individuals. By combining these psychological modalities within a comprehensive treatment plan, clinicians and mental health professionals can address the diverse and complex factors contributing to social withdrawal.

Social Reintegration Programs

Social reintegration programs stand as a cornerstone in addressing hikikomori, aiming to facilitate the gradual transition of individuals from a state of isolation to active participation in society. This section delves into the intricacies of social reintegration strategies and their significance in the comprehensive treatment of hikikomori.

Community Engagement Initiatives. Social reintegration often begins at the community level. Initiatives that foster community engagement, such as local events, workshops, and support groups, create opportunities for individuals to reconnect with their immediate surroundings. These initiatives aim to build a sense of belonging and reduce the barriers to social participation.

Volunteer and Skill Development Programs. Participation in volunteer activities and skill development programs offers hikikomori individuals a structured and purposeful way to engage with the community. By contributing to social causes or acquiring new skills, individuals can regain a sense of accomplishment and gradually rebuild their confidence in interacting with others.

Employment Support Services. Integrating hikikomori individuals into the workforce is a pivotal aspect of social reintegration. Employment support services encompass vocational training, job placement assistance, and workplace accommodations. Meaningful employment not only provides financial independence but also fosters a sense of purpose and social connection.

Educational Reintegration Programs. For those whose withdrawal is linked to educational challenges, educational reintegration programs offer tailored solutions. These may include flexible learning environments, academic counseling, and mentorship programs. Adaptive educational models aim to address the unique needs of hikikomori individuals, promoting a positive reconnection with learning.

Peer Mentorship and Support Networks. Peer mentorship programs play a crucial role in social reintegration by connecting individuals with shared experiences. Establishing support networks where peers who have successfully navigated hikikomori offer guidance and encouragement creates a supportive environment for those on the path to recovery.

Structured Social Activities. Structured social activities provide a gradual and non-threatening entry into social interactions. These activities, ranging from group outings to hobby clubs, offer a controlled environment where individuals can practice social skills, build relationships, and increase their comfort levels in various social settings.

Family Involvement and Counseling. Recognizing the impact of family dynamics, social reintegration programs often involve families in the process. Family counseling sessions provide a platform for open communication, addressing concerns, and developing strategies to support the individual's reintegration into social life.

Community Awareness Campaigns. Beyond individual interventions, community awareness campaigns play a vital role in reducing stigma and fostering understanding. By educating the community about hikikomori and its complexities, these campaigns contribute to a more supportive and inclusive environment for individuals seeking to reintegrate into society.

Social reintegration programs operate on the principle that successful reintegration is a gradual and personalized journey. Tailoring interventions to the unique needs and preferences of hikikomori individuals is essential for fostering sustainable social connections and empowering them to reclaim active roles within their communities. As we navigate the landscape of social reintegration, it becomes evident that a holistic and collaborative approach is fundamental to the success of these programs.

Success Stories and Testimonials

Within the realm of hikikomori intervention, the power of success stories and testimonials emerges as a poignant force in inspiring hope and catalyzing positive change. It is important to report the narratives of individuals who have successfully navigated the challenges of social withdrawal, highlighting the diverse pathways to recovery.

Personal Narratives of Recovery. Success stories serve as beacons of inspiration, providing first-hand accounts of individuals who have triumphed over hikikomori. These narratives offer insights into the various strategies, coping mechanisms, and support systems that proved instrumental in their journey toward recovery. By sharing personal experiences, these stories resonate with those currently facing social withdrawal, instilling a sense of possibility and resilience.

Peer Support Networks. Testimonials within peer support networks contribute to the communal understanding of hikikomori and its complexities. Individuals who have overcome social withdrawal often become advocates within these networks, sharing their stories to provide guidance and encouragement to others. Peer support fosters a sense of camaraderie, breaking the isolation that hikikomori individuals may experience.

Family Testimonies and Insights. The impact of hikikomori extends beyond the individual to their families and caregivers. Testimonials from family members offer a unique perspective on the challenges faced and the strategies employed in supporting a loved one through recovery. These insights provide valuable guidance for families navigating the complexities of hikikomori, emphasizing the importance of empathy and understanding.

Educational Success Stories. Within the context of hikikomori and education, success stories from individuals who have successfully reintegrated into educational settings provide valuable insights. These narratives shed light on innovative educational models, supportive environments, and personalized approaches that have contributed to academic success and personal growth. Such stories become blueprints for reforming educational systems to accommodate the needs of hikikomori individuals.

Community Integration Narratives. Testimonials focused on community integration underscore the significance of local initiatives and community involvement. Individuals who have successfully reconnected with their communities share stories of acceptance, understanding, and the positive impact of community-based interventions.

These narratives emphasize the role of collective efforts in creating an inclusive and supportive social environment.

Advocacy Success Stories. Success stories within the realm of hikikomori advocacy highlight the transformative power of awareness campaigns, anti-stigma initiatives, and policy advocacy. Individuals who have actively contributed to destigmatizing social withdrawal share their experiences, providing insights into the impact of advocacy in shaping public perception and fostering empathy.

Through the exploration of success stories and testimonials, this section aims to illuminate the diverse avenues to recovery and reintegration. By presenting real-life examples of resilience, perseverance, and transformation, we seek to instill a sense of optimism and possibility within the broader discourse on hikikomori intervention. These narratives not only celebrate individual triumphs but also contribute to a collective understanding that inspires informed, compassionate, and effective approaches to addressing social withdrawal.

In the bustling city of Tokyo, Ken's journey through hikikomori was a labyrinth of isolation and uncertainty. At the age of 23, Ken found himself immersed in the virtual cocoon of his room, grappling with the challenges of social withdrawal. The glow of screens became his solace, shielding him from the complexities of the outside world.

Ken's turning point came through an online support community tailored for individuals experiencing hikikomori. There, he discovered a tapestry of narratives, each thread weaving tales of struggle, resilience, and recovery. Drawn to the stories of those who had successfully navigated social withdrawal, Ken found a glimmer of hope and inspiration.

Emboldened by the sense of camaraderie within the online community, Ken began engaging in discussions, sharing his own experiences, and forming connections with individuals facing similar challenges. Peer support became a cornerstone of his recovery, as the shared journey towards reconnection created a web of understanding and encouragement.

Motivated to bridge the gap between virtual and real-world interactions, Ken embraced digital skill-building programs. Online courses focused on communication, self-expression, and emotional intelligence empowered him with the tools needed to navigate face-to-face interactions with increased confidence.

Ken's family played a pivotal role in his recovery. Their unwavering support and efforts to understand the challenges of hikikomori fostered an environment of acceptance and empathy. Family testimonies within the online community offered insights into effective coping strategies and communication patterns, creating a shared language for healing.

As Ken gradually reentered the physical world, community integration became a priority. Local initiatives and meet-up groups facilitated by the online community provided safe spaces for him to practice social interactions. Community support proved instrumental in dismantling the walls of isolation that had confined him for so long.

Embracing innovative educational models, Ken enrolled in a flexible online education program. The personalized approach allowed him to pursue academic interests at his own pace, creating a conducive environment for learning without the overwhelming pressures of traditional schooling.

Inspired by his own transformation, Ken became an advocate within the hikikomori community. He shared his story in awareness campaigns and contributed to anti-stigma initiatives, aiming to reshape public perception. Ken's journey from isolation to advocacy showcased the transformative potential of collective efforts in fostering understanding and empathy.

Ken's success story is a testament to the resilience that lies within individuals facing hikikomori. His journey, marked by the power of peer support, digital skill-building, family understanding, community integration, educational reintegration, and advocacy, serves as a beacon for those navigating the challenging terrain of social withdrawal. Ken's triumph is not only a personal victory but also a contribution to the broader narrative of hope and possibility in the realm of hikikomori recovery.

CHAPTER 5
BRIDGING THE GAP

Importance of Community Involvement
In the intricate tapestry of hikikomori intervention, community involvement emerges as a linchpin in fostering understanding, acceptance, and support. Community engagement is an essential component in addressing social withdrawal.

Creating a Supportive Ecosystem. Communities serve as the bedrock for creating a supportive ecosystem that surrounds individuals experiencing hikikomori. The involvement of neighbors, local organizations, and community leaders fosters an environment of empathy, reducing the stigma associated with social withdrawal. By embracing those affected, communities contribute to the creation of a safety net that facilitates reintegration.

Raising Awareness and Understanding. Community involvement plays a pivotal role in raising awareness and promoting a deeper understanding of hikikomori. Educational campaigns within local schools, workplaces, and public spaces create platforms for dispelling myths, sharing information, and fostering open conversations. As awareness spreads, communities become better equipped to recognize signs of social withdrawal and offer informed support.

Local Support Groups and Initiatives. The establishment of local support groups and initiatives tailored to hikikomori individuals provides avenues for shared experiences and mutual encouragement. These groups, whether online or in-person, serve as spaces for individuals to connect, discuss challenges, and access resources. The communal aspect of support groups combats isolation and reinforces a sense of belonging.

Community-based Interventions. Tailoring interventions to the specific needs of a community is crucial in addressing hikikomori. Localized initiatives, such as workshops, seminars, and counseling services, contribute to the accessibility of support. Community-based interventions acknowledge the unique cultural and social context in which hikikomori individuals exist, ensuring that solutions resonate with the community's values and norms.

Fostering Inclusive Spaces. Community involvement thrives on the creation of inclusive spaces where hikikomori individuals feel accepted and supported. Businesses, recreational facilities, and public spaces can play a role in adapting environments to accommodate those experiencing social withdrawal. The active encouragement of inclusive practices ensures that individuals are welcomed without judgment.

Collaboration with Mental Health Professionals. Engaging mental health professionals within the community establishes a collaborative approach to hikikomori intervention. By forging partnerships with local counselors, therapists, and support services, communities strengthen their capacity to provide comprehensive and sustained assistance. This collaborative model facilitates early intervention and ongoing support.

Empowering Families and Caregivers. Community involvement extends to empowering families and caregivers who play a crucial role in the lives of hikikomori individuals. Workshops, support networks, and educational programs aimed at families enhance their understanding of social withdrawal and equip them with effective coping strategies. The empowerment of families contributes to a more compassionate and informed community response.

In essence, the importance of community involvement lies in its ability to create a web of understanding, acceptance, and support around hikikomori individuals. By actively engaging communities, we pave the way for a more inclusive and empathetic society that recognizes the complexities of social withdrawal and actively works towards bridging the gap between isolation and reconnection.

Building Support Networks for Hikikomori Individuals

In the intricate landscape of hikikomori intervention, the establishment of robust support networks is a cornerstone for fostering reconnection and resilience. This section meticulously explores the strategies and dynamics involved in building effective support networks tailored to the unique needs of individuals experiencing social withdrawal.

Community Involvement Initiatives. Initiating community involvement programs designed specifically for hikikomori individuals is a pivotal step. These initiatives may include local workshops, support groups, and events that provide safe and inclusive spaces for individuals to gradually reintegrate into communal activities. Collaborating with mental health professionals, educators, and community leaders ensures a holistic approach to support.

Peer Support Platforms. Creating dedicated peer support platforms, both online and offline, is instrumental in fostering connections among individuals facing similar challenges. Online forums, chat groups, or scheduled meet-ups offer spaces where hikikomori individuals can share experiences, offer mutual support, and exchange coping strategies. Peer support serves as a powerful antidote to the isolation often associated with social withdrawal.

Mentorship Programs. Establishing mentorship programs pairs individuals on their recovery journey with mentors who have successfully overcome hikikomori. These mentors, often individuals with similar experiences, provide guidance, encouragement, and practical insights. Mentorship programs offer a structured framework for building one-on-one relationships and creating a sense of accountability within the support network.

Family Support Workshops. Recognizing the crucial role of families in the recovery process, hosting support workshops tailored for families and caregivers is essential. These workshops focus on enhancing understanding, communication, and coping strategies within the familial environment. Expert-led discussions and shared experiences contribute to a supportive family network that complements the broader support ecosystem.

Collaboration with Educational Institutions. Engaging educational institutions is vital in creating support networks for hikikomori individuals within academic settings. Collaborative efforts can involve the development of specialized support services, awareness programs, and peer-led initiatives within schools and universities. Integration into educational environments often serves as a catalyst for social reintegration.

Employment Assistance Programs. Facilitating employment assistance programs addresses the practical challenges of hikikomori individuals seeking to reintegrate into the workforce. Collaborating with businesses, career counselors, and vocational training centers, these programs provide tailored support, skill development opportunities, and employment pathways, empowering individuals to regain financial independence.

Community Mentoring Circles. Community mentoring circles bring together individuals at various stages of recovery, fostering a sense of belonging and collective growth. These circles, guided by experienced facilitators, provide a structured yet informal environment for sharing stories, discussing challenges, and celebrating milestones. The diverse perspectives within the circle contribute to a rich tapestry of support.

Building effective support networks for hikikomori individuals necessitates a comprehensive, community-driven approach. By intertwining peer support, family engagement, educational collaboration, and employment assistance, these networks become a multifaceted safety net that nurtures reconnection, resilience, and lasting recovery. This book underscores the importance of intentional, collaborative efforts in constructing support networks that cater to the unique needs and aspirations of individuals navigating the complexities of social withdrawal.

Community Initiatives and Best Practices

In the pursuit of addressing hikikomori, community initiatives stand as pillars of support, actively contributing to the creation of inclusive environments that foster understanding and reintegration. This section explores exemplary community initiatives and best practices that have proven effective in bridging the gap for individuals experiencing social withdrawal.

Community Awareness Programs. Successful community initiatives often begin with raising awareness. Programs that educate community members about hikikomori, its nuances, and the challenges faced by individuals, play a crucial role in dispelling misconceptions and reducing stigma. Awareness campaigns may involve workshops, seminars, and informational materials distributed across schools, workplaces, and public spaces.

Peer Mentorship Programs. Implementing peer mentorship programs within communities has demonstrated significant positive impacts. Individuals who have successfully emerged from hikikomori can serve as mentors to those currently facing social withdrawal. These mentors offer guidance, empathy, and practical insights, creating a supportive network that understands the unique challenges of the journey.

Community Support Centers. Establishing dedicated community support centers provides tangible resources for individuals dealing with hikikomori. These centers can offer a range of services, including counseling, vocational guidance, and skill-building workshops. The physical presence of these centers within communities acts as a visible symbol of support, encouraging those in need to seek assistance.

Local Events and Activities. Engaging individuals in local events and activities facilitates gradual reintegration into the community. Community-driven events, such as art exhibitions, cultural festivals, or volunteer initiatives, provide opportunities for social interaction in a non-threatening environment. Participation in these activities fosters a sense of belonging and purpose.

Collaboration with Educational Institutions. Best practices often involve close collaboration between community initiatives and educational institutions. Schools and universities can play a pivotal role in identifying and supporting individuals at risk of hikikomori. Educational reforms that prioritize mental health, reduce academic pressures, and create inclusive environments contribute to a holistic approach in addressing social withdrawal.

Employment Support Programs. Integrating hikikomori individuals into the workforce is a critical component of community initiatives. Employment support programs can include vocational training, job placement assistance, and initiatives promoting workplace inclusivity. Meaningful employment not only provides financial independence but also contributes to a sense of purpose and social connection.

Crisis Intervention and Hotline Services. Establishing crisis intervention and hotline services ensures that immediate support is available for individuals in acute distress. Community-driven hotlines staffed by trained professionals provide a lifeline for those grappling with hikikomori, offering immediate assistance, crisis intervention, and referrals to relevant support services.

Family Support Networks. Acknowledging the integral role of families, community initiatives can establish family support networks. These networks facilitate the exchange of experiences, coping strategies, and emotional support among families dealing with hikikomori. Workshops and support groups tailored for families contribute to a holistic approach in addressing the challenges posed by social withdrawal.

Through the implementation of these best practices, communities can actively contribute to dismantling the barriers associated with hikikomori. By fostering understanding, offering tangible support, and creating environments that prioritize empathy and inclusivity, community initiatives play a pivotal role in bridging the gap and paving the way for the reintegration of individuals experiencing social withdrawal.

CHAPTER 6
EDUCATIONAL SYSTEMS
AND HIKIKOMORI

School-related Stressors and Withdrawal
The intersection of hikikomori and educational systems reveals a complex interplay of factors that contribute to social withdrawal among young individuals. This section meticulously examines the school-related stressors that can serve as catalysts for hikikomori, shedding light on the nuances of this critical relationship.

Academic Pressure and Performance Expectations. Hikikomori often finds its roots in the intense academic pressures prevalent within educational systems. The relentless pursuit of high academic performance, coupled with societal expectations and competition, can create an overwhelming environment for students. Fear of failure, coupled with the stigma associated with academic underachievement, may drive some individuals to retreat from the academic sphere.

Social Dynamics and Peer Relationships. The social landscape within educational institutions plays a pivotal role in hikikomori. For some individuals, challenges in forming and maintaining peer relationships can be significant stressors. Bullying, social exclusion, or the perceived inability to conform to societal norms can lead to a sense of isolation, prompting withdrawal as a coping mechanism.

Educational Structure and Conformity. The rigid structure of traditional educational systems may not align with the diverse needs and learning styles of every student. Individuals who struggle to conform to the standardized educational model may experience frustration and alienation. The inability to thrive within the established educational framework may contribute to a sense of failure, fostering the desire to escape from the academic environment.

Testing and Examination Pressures. High-stakes testing and examinations add another layer of stress to the educational experience. The intense focus on standardized testing can create an environment of anxiety and fear of academic evaluation. For some individuals, the pressure associated with exams becomes a significant trigger for social withdrawal, as the prospect of failure looms large.

Teacher-Student Dynamics. The quality of relationships between students and teachers can influence the emotional well-being of students. Harsh disciplinary measures, lack of understanding, or inadequate support from educators may contribute to a negative school environment. In such cases, students may perceive the educational setting as adversarial, pushing them towards withdrawal as a means of self-preservation.

Cultural and Societal Expectations. Cultural and societal expectations regarding academic success and career paths can place immense pressure on students. The expectation to conform to predetermined trajectories may clash with individual aspirations and capabilities. This dissonance can fuel feelings of inadequacy and frustration, becoming potential precursors to hikikomori.

Understanding the intricacies of school-related stressors is fundamental in addressing hikikomori within the educational context. By identifying and addressing these stressors, educational institutions can play a pivotal role in creating environments that foster the well-being and holistic development of students, thereby mitigating the risk of social withdrawal.

Innovative Educational Models

In addressing the intricate intersection of hikikomori and educational systems, a pivotal consideration is the exploration of innovative educational models. It is necessary to consider unconventional approaches that have shown promise in accommodating the unique needs of individuals experiencing social withdrawal.

Flexible Online Learning Platforms. Innovative educational models often incorporate flexible online learning platforms that cater to the diverse learning styles and paces of hikikomori individuals. These platforms provide a supportive environment where individuals can engage with educational content at their own rhythm, alleviating the stressors associated with traditional classroom settings.

Personalized Learning Plans. Recognizing the individualized nature of hikikomori experiences, innovative educational models embrace personalized learning plans. Tailored to the specific needs, interests, and strengths of each student, these plans empower individuals to take ownership of their educational journey. Personalization fosters a sense of autonomy and self-efficacy, crucial components in rekindling a positive relationship with learning.

Mentorship Programs. Mentorship programs within educational models offer a one-on-one support system, pairing hikikomori individuals with mentors who provide guidance, encouragement, and a sense of accountability. The mentor-student relationship extends beyond academic assistance, encompassing holistic support to navigate the challenges of both education and social reintegration.

Experiential Learning Opportunities. To address the disconnect between traditional educational settings and the practicalities of real-world experiences, innovative models incorporate experiential learning opportunities. Field trips, internships, and project-based learning initiatives enable hikikomori individuals to apply academic knowledge in real-life contexts, fostering a deeper and more meaningful engagement with education.

Community-Based Learning Environments. Departing from the conventional classroom structure, some innovative models advocate for community-based learning environments. These settings encourage collaboration, social interaction, and shared learning experiences within the local community. The emphasis on community integration aligns with the broader goal of reestablishing connections beyond the confines of social withdrawal.

Life Skills and Social Integration Programs. Recognizing the importance of equipping hikikomori individuals with practical life skills, innovative educational models often integrate programs that focus on social integration, communication skills, and emotional intelligence. These programs go beyond traditional academic curricula, addressing the holistic development needed for successful reintegration into society.

Multidisciplinary Approaches. Multidisciplinary approaches bring together various academic disciplines, combining elements of arts, sciences, humanities, and vocational training. By offering a diverse range of subjects and learning pathways, these models cater to the varied interests of hikikomori individuals, promoting a sense of purpose and relevance in their educational pursuits.

In essence, innovative educational models seek to create a learning environment that not only accommodates the specific challenges posed by hikikomori but also nurtures individual growth and reintegration. By reimagining traditional educational structures and embracing flexibility, personalization, and community involvement, these models strive to empower individuals to overcome the hurdles of social withdrawal and embark on a meaningful educational journey.

Educational Policies and Reforms

In addressing the intersection of hikikomori and educational systems, the implementation of thoughtful policies and reforms becomes a crucial component. This section described the landscape of educational policies designed to recognize and accommodate the needs of individuals facing social withdrawal.

Inclusive Education Policies. Developing inclusive education policies is essential for creating a supportive environment within mainstream educational settings. These policies should aim to recognize the diverse learning styles and needs of hikikomori individuals. Inclusive practices involve adapting teaching methods, providing additional support, and fostering a culture of understanding among educators and peers.

Flexible Learning Environments. Recognizing the individualized nature of hikikomori experiences, educational reforms should prioritize the establishment of flexible learning environments. This could include alternative learning paths, personalized curricula, and adaptable scheduling to accommodate the unique challenges and pace of individuals reintegrating into educational settings.

Mental Health Support in Schools. Integrating mental health support within the educational framework is imperative. Educational policies should advocate for the presence of mental health professionals in schools, equipped to identify early signs of social withdrawal and provide timely interventions. Training educators to recognize and address mental health challenges contributes to a holistic approach to student well-being.

Anti-Bullying Initiatives. Hikikomori individuals may have experienced bullying or social challenges that contributed to their withdrawal. Implementing and enforcing anti-bullying initiatives within schools creates a safer and more inclusive environment. Policies should promote a culture of respect, understanding, and empathy, fostering an atmosphere where students feel accepted and supported.

Peer Mentorship Programs. Educational reforms can introduce peer mentorship programs where students who have successfully navigated hikikomori and reintegrated into school life serve as mentors. These programs provide valuable peer support, encouragement, and guidance, creating a sense of community within the school environment.

Collaboration with Mental Health Services. Educational policies should prioritize collaboration between schools and external mental health services. This partnership ensures a seamless transition for hikikomori individuals seeking professional mental health support. Clear referral pathways, open communication channels, and joint initiatives contribute to a comprehensive and integrated support system.

Flexible Graduation Requirements. Recognizing that hikikomori individuals may have interrupted academic trajectories, educational policies should include flexible graduation requirements. This flexibility allows individuals to progress academically at their own pace, acknowledging their unique circumstances and providing opportunities for academic success.

Parental Involvement Policies. Educational reforms should emphasize the importance of parental involvement in addressing hikikomori. Policies can encourage regular communication between schools and parents, ensuring a collaborative approach to support. Workshops and resources for parents on understanding hikikomori and fostering positive family dynamics contribute to a holistic support structure.

Culturally Competent Education. Educational policies must be culturally competent, recognizing that the experience of hikikomori may vary across different cultural contexts. Tailoring policies to address cultural nuances ensures that interventions are sensitive and effective, promoting inclusivity and understanding.

In essence, educational policies and reforms play a pivotal role in creating an environment that fosters the reintegration of hikikomori individuals into educational settings. By addressing the unique needs of these individuals and promoting a culture of inclusivity and support, educational systems can become instrumental agents of positive change in the journey towards overcoming social withdrawal.

CHAPTER 7
HIKIKOMORI AND MENTAL HEALTH

Linking Hikikomori to Mental Health Disorders
Understanding the intricate relationship between hikikomori and mental health is essential for developing effective intervention strategies. In this section, we explore the connections between social withdrawal and various mental health disorders, shedding light on the complex interplay of psychological factors.

Social Withdrawal as a Coping Mechanism. Hikikomori often emerges as a coping mechanism in response to overwhelming stressors and challenges. Individuals may retreat from social interactions to create a perceived sense of safety and control. Examining the roots of hikikomori reveals its role as a manifestation of underlying psychological distress, with withdrawal serving as a protective mechanism against external pressures.

Anxiety Disorders and Social Withdrawal. Anxiety disorders, characterized by excessive worry and fear, are frequently intertwined with hikikomori. Social situations may trigger intense anxiety, prompting individuals to withdraw to alleviate distress. Understanding the specific anxiety triggers and developing targeted interventions is crucial for addressing the underlying causes of hikikomori associated with anxiety disorders.

Depressive Symptoms and Isolation. Depression often accompanies hikikomori, creating a cycle of isolation and emotional withdrawal. Feelings of hopelessness, fatigue, and a lack of interest in once-enjoyed activities contribute to the reluctance to engage with the outside world. Addressing depressive symptoms becomes integral in breaking the cycle of withdrawal and fostering a path towards recovery.

Autism Spectrum Disorders and Social Challenges. Individuals with autism spectrum disorders (ASD) may face unique social challenges that contribute to hikikomori. Difficulty in navigating social cues and forming connections can lead to withdrawal as a coping strategy. Tailoring interventions to accommodate the specific needs of individuals with ASD is essential for fostering social engagement and integration.

Obsessive-Compulsive Features and Rituals. Hikikomori individuals may exhibit obsessive-compulsive features, incorporating rituals and routines as a means of managing anxiety. These features can contribute to a rigid lifestyle centered around the safety of the home environment. Recognizing the role of obsessive-compulsive tendencies is crucial for designing interventions that address the underlying psychological mechanisms.

Trauma and Post-Traumatic Stress. Hikikomori can also be linked to experiences of trauma and post-traumatic stress. Individuals may withdraw as a response to traumatic events, creating a self-imposed isolation to avoid triggers. Trauma-informed interventions are vital in providing support tailored to the unique needs of individuals with hikikomori rooted in traumatic experiences.

Understanding the mental health dimensions of hikikomori involves recognizing that social withdrawal is often a symptom rather than a stand-alone condition. By delving into the specific mental health disorders associated with hikikomori, we pave the way for targeted interventions that address the underlying psychological factors, promoting a holistic approach to recovery.

Dual Diagnosis and Co-occurring Conditions

Understanding the intricate relationship between hikikomori and mental health necessitates a nuanced exploration of dual diagnosis and co-occurring conditions. This book delves into the complexities of individuals facing both hikikomori and concurrent mental health disorders, shedding light on the interconnected nature of these challenges.

Prevalence of Dual Diagnosis. Hikikomori often coexists with various mental health disorders, amplifying the complexity of the phenomenon. Dual diagnosis refers to the presence of both social withdrawal and a diagnosable mental health condition. The prevalence of dual diagnosis underscores the need for integrated and comprehensive approaches that address both aspects of an individual's well-being.

Common Co-occurring Mental Health Disorders. Individuals experiencing hikikomori may simultaneously grapple with a spectrum of mental health disorders. Depression, anxiety disorders, social anxiety, obsessive-compulsive disorder (OCD), and post-traumatic stress disorder (PTSD) are among the commonly observed co-occurring conditions. Each disorder contributes to the challenges of social withdrawal, creating a layered and intricate experience for the individual.

Bidirectional Impact. The relationship between hikikomori and mental health is often bidirectional. Social withdrawal can be both a symptom and a consequence of mental health disorders.

For instance, an individual with untreated depression may withdraw socially, while prolonged social withdrawal itself can contribute to the development or exacerbation of mental health conditions.

Challenges in Diagnosis and Treatment. Dual diagnosis poses challenges in both diagnosis and treatment. The concealment of hikikomori behaviors and the stigma associated with mental health conditions may impede accurate diagnosis. Additionally, treating co-occurring disorders requires a holistic approach that considers the interplay between social withdrawal and mental health, emphasizing the importance of integrated therapeutic strategies.

Impact on Recovery Journeys. Individuals with dual diagnosis often face unique hurdles on their journey to recovery. Addressing hikikomori and mental health disorders concurrently requires a coordinated and collaborative effort from mental health professionals, social support networks, and treatment providers. Tailoring interventions to the specific needs of individuals with dual diagnosis is essential for fostering comprehensive recovery.

Integrated Mental Health Support. Recognizing the intertwined nature of hikikomori and mental health, interventions must prioritize integrated mental health support. This includes collaborative treatment plans that address both the social withdrawal aspect and the underlying mental health conditions. Psychoeducation, counseling, medication management, and peer support all play crucial roles in this integrated approach.

Future Directions in Research. The exploration of dual diagnosis and co-occurring conditions within the hikikomori context necessitates ongoing research to unravel the intricate dynamics. Understanding the specific patterns and prevalence of co-occurring disorders informs targeted interventions and contributes to the development of tailored support systems.

Recognizing and addressing dual diagnosis and co-occurring conditions within the framework of hikikomori is pivotal for designing effective and empathetic interventions. By comprehensively understanding the intersection of social withdrawal and mental health, we pave the way for holistic recovery journeys that prioritize the diverse needs of individuals facing these interconnected challenges.

Integrating Mental Health Support

In the intricate landscape of hikikomori, the integration of mental health support stands as a cornerstone for understanding, addressing, and fostering recovery from social withdrawal. This section delves into the nuanced strategies and considerations essential for weaving mental health support seamlessly into the fabric of hikikomori intervention.

Holistic Assessment and Diagnosis. The first step in integrating mental health support involves a comprehensive and holistic assessment of individuals experiencing hikikomori. Mental health professionals employ thorough diagnostic evaluations, considering not only the symptoms of social withdrawal but also underlying mental health conditions that may contribute to or result from hikikomori.

Individualized Treatment Plans. Recognizing the diversity of experiences within the hikikomori spectrum, mental health professionals collaborate with individuals to develop individualized treatment plans. These plans encompass evidence-based therapeutic modalities, addressing both the social withdrawal symptoms and any co-occurring mental health disorders. Cognitive-behavioral therapy, exposure therapy, and mindfulness-based interventions are tailored to the unique needs of each individual.

Family-Centered Interventions. As families play a crucial role in the hikikomori narrative, integrating mental health support extends to family-centered interventions. Family therapy becomes a space for open communication, conflict resolution, and the development of supportive structures. Understanding the familial dynamics surrounding social withdrawal is paramount in creating a conducive environment for recovery.

Crisis Intervention and Emergency Services. Acknowledging the potential for crisis situations, mental health support includes crisis intervention and access to emergency services. Crisis hotlines, mobile crisis teams, and emergency response plans are integral components, ensuring immediate assistance for individuals facing acute distress or heightened anxiety.

Psychoeducation and Skill-building. Empowering individuals with knowledge about mental health and equipping them with coping skills is fundamental. Psychoeducation initiatives provide information about social anxiety, depression, and other mental health conditions associated with hikikomori. Skill-building programs focus on developing coping mechanisms, resilience, and social skills essential for reintegration.

Long-Term Follow-up and Monitoring. The journey of hikikomori recovery is ongoing, requiring long-term follow-up and monitoring. Mental health professionals collaborate with individuals to assess progress, address evolving needs, and make adjustments to treatment plans as necessary. Consistent follow-up ensures sustained support and prevents relapse.

Collaboration with Community Resources. Integrating mental health support extends beyond clinical settings to collaboration with community resources. Community mental health services, peer support groups, and community-based organizations contribute to a holistic support network, fostering a seamless transition from formal treatment to ongoing community engagement.

Destigmatization Initiatives. An integral aspect of integrating mental health support is the destigmatization of seeking help. Advocacy and awareness campaigns focused on dismantling stigmas surrounding mental health and social withdrawal contribute to creating an environment where individuals feel comfortable seeking assistance.

By weaving mental health support into the fabric of hikikomori intervention, this comprehensive approach acknowledges the interconnected nature of social withdrawal and mental health. As we navigate this integration, the goal is to provide multifaceted support that addresses the complexities of hikikomori, fosters recovery, and promotes lasting mental well-being.

CHAPTER 8
FAMILY DYNAMICS
AND COPING MECHANISMS

Impact on Families and Caregivers
The journey through hikikomori is not a solitary experience confined to the individual; its ripples extend to families and caregivers who grapple with the complexities of social withdrawal. It is necessary to analyze the profound impact that hikikomori has on families and explores the dynamics that unfold within the familial context.

Emotional Toll on Families. The onset of hikikomori often brings a wave of emotions within families—confusion, worry, guilt, and a sense of helplessness. Families may experience a profound emotional toll as they witness a loved one withdrawing from social interactions and daily life. Understanding the emotional landscape is crucial for developing empathetic support systems.

Communication Breakdowns. Hikikomori can lead to significant communication breakdowns within families. Individuals experiencing social withdrawal may struggle to articulate their feelings, while family members may find it challenging to comprehend the reasons behind the withdrawal. This communication gap can intensify feelings of frustration and isolation on both sides.

Stigmatization and Social Isolation. Families often grapple with societal stigmatization, with the burden of judgment and misunderstanding impacting their daily lives. The fear of social judgment can lead to families withdrawing from their own support networks, exacerbating feelings of

SIMPLE SHORT BOOKS 63

isolation. Addressing stigmatization is crucial for creating an environment that nurtures understanding and acceptance.

Roles and Responsibilities Shift. Hikikomori often necessitates a reevaluation of roles and responsibilities within families. Caregivers may take on additional responsibilities, balancing support for the individual experiencing withdrawal with the demands of everyday life. Understanding the shifting dynamics and establishing clear communication about roles is vital for maintaining family equilibrium.

Financial and Practical Strain. The practical implications of hikikomori can extend to financial strain, especially if the individual is unable to participate in education or employment. Families may face challenges in providing the necessary support while managing the associated costs. Addressing financial concerns requires a holistic approach that considers both short-term and long-term strategies.

Coping Strategies for Families. Families often develop coping mechanisms to navigate the challenges of hikikomori. These strategies may include seeking professional guidance, participating in support groups, and fostering open communication within the family unit. Understanding and implementing effective coping strategies can contribute to the overall well-being of both the individual and the family.

Seeking Professional Support. Recognizing the complexities of hikikomori, families may seek professional support from mental health professionals, therapists, and counselors. Professional guidance can assist families in understanding the underlying factors contributing to social withdrawal and provide strategies for fostering a supportive environment.

Encouraging Incremental Progress. Families play a crucial role in encouraging incremental progress. Celebrating small victories, no matter how minor, can contribute to the individual's sense of accomplishment and motivation for further reintegration. Patience and encouragement become essential elements in supporting the gradual journey toward recovery.

This exploration of the impact on families lays the groundwork for understanding the intricate dynamics surrounding hikikomori. By acknowledging the emotional, communicative, and practical challenges families face, we can pave the way for developing comprehensive and empathetic support systems that address the needs of both individuals experiencing social withdrawal and those who care for them.

Coping Strategies for Families

Navigating the complexities of hikikomori involves not only the individuals experiencing social withdrawal but also their families and caregivers. This section describes coping strategies that families can employ to provide support, understanding, and a conducive environment for the recovery of their loved ones facing hikikomori.

Open Communication Channels. Establishing open and non-judgmental communication channels is foundational. Families are encouraged to create an environment where individuals facing hikikomori feel comfortable expressing their thoughts and emotions. Honest conversations foster mutual understanding and lay the groundwork for collaborative solutions.

Educate and Seek Information. Education is a powerful tool for families dealing with hikikomori. Understanding the nuances of social withdrawal, its potential causes, and the available support resources equips families with the knowledge needed to navigate the journey effectively. Seeking information from reputable sources and mental health professionals is crucial.

Professional Guidance. Involving mental health professionals in the process is instrumental. Seeking the expertise of psychologists, counselors, and therapists can provide families with insights into the psychological aspects of hikikomori. Professional guidance helps families develop tailored strategies and interventions that align with the unique needs of their loved ones.

Establishing Routine and Structure. Creating a sense of routine and structure within the household can be stabilizing. Consistent daily schedules, including meal times, chores, and family activities, provide a framework that contributes to a predictable environment. This predictability can be reassuring for individuals experiencing hikikomori.

Encourage Incremental Steps. Encouraging small, incremental steps towards social engagement is essential. Families can work with their loved ones to set achievable goals, gradually increasing exposure to social situations. Celebrating these milestones fosters a sense of accomplishment and reinforces positive behavior.

Balancing Independence and Support. Striking a balance between fostering independence and providing support is a delicate task. Families should encourage autonomy while remaining available for assistance when needed. Empowering individuals facing hikikomori to make decisions about their recovery journey enhances their sense of agency.

Family Therapy. Family therapy is a valuable resource for addressing interpersonal dynamics and strengthening familial bonds. Engaging in therapy sessions as a family unit allows for the exploration of communication patterns, conflict resolution, and the development of strategies that contribute to a supportive and understanding family environment.

Self-Care for Caregivers. The well-being of caregivers is paramount. Family members supporting individuals with hikikomori may experience their own emotional challenges. Implementing self-care practices, seeking support from their own social networks, and recognizing the importance of their mental health contribute to a resilient support system.

Community Engagement. Connecting with other families facing similar challenges can be reassuring. Joining support groups or community initiatives focused on hikikomori creates opportunities for families to share experiences, insights, and coping strategies. The sense of community can alleviate feelings of isolation.

Cultivate Patience and Understanding. Patience is a virtue in the process of coping with hikikomori. Families are encouraged to cultivate understanding, recognizing that recovery is a gradual journey. Celebrating progress, no matter how small, and maintaining a hopeful outlook contribute to a positive family environment.

By embracing these coping strategies, families can play a vital role in supporting their loved ones through the challenges of hikikomori. The collaborative efforts of families, coupled with professional guidance and a compassionate approach, contribute to the creation of a resilient and understanding foundation for the recovery journey.

Family Testimonies and Insights
In the intricate tapestry of hikikomori, family dynamics play a crucial role in both the emergence and resolution of social withdrawal. This section delves into the invaluable perspectives provided by family testimonies, offering a nuanced understanding of the challenges faced, coping strategies employed, and the transformative impact of familial support in the journey toward recovery.

Impact on Families and Caregivers. Family members often find themselves grappling with a myriad of emotions when a loved one experiences hikikomori. Feelings of confusion, frustration, and concern may permeate the household as they witness the withdrawal of their family member. Family testimonies shed light on the emotional toll hikikomori can take on those in caregiving roles, providing insight into the need for compassion and resilience within the family unit.

Coping Strategies for Families. Within the realm of hikikomori, families develop unique coping strategies to navigate the challenges posed by social withdrawal. These may include fostering open communication, seeking professional guidance, and creating a supportive environment that encourages the individual to express their feelings without judgment. Family testimonies become reservoirs of wisdom, offering practical insights into coping mechanisms that have proven effective in specific contexts.

Family Testimonies and Insights. Real-life accounts from families who have weathered the storm of hikikomori provide a personal and relatable dimension to the challenges faced. These testimonies share the emotional journey of families, from the initial discovery of social withdrawal to the collaborative efforts taken toward recovery. Insights gleaned from these narratives include the importance of patience, the power of understanding, and the role of consistent support in fostering an environment conducive to healing.

Balancing Boundaries and Support. Family testimonies often illuminate the delicate balance between respecting an individual's need for space and providing unwavering support. Families share their experiences of setting boundaries to encourage gradual reintegration while maintaining a safety net of support. Understanding the fine line between offering assistance and allowing autonomy becomes a crucial aspect of the familial journey through hikikomori

Holistic Approaches to Support. Family testimonies also underscore the significance of adopting holistic approaches to support. This includes addressing not only the symptoms of hikikomori but also the underlying factors contributing to social withdrawal. Families share insights into seeking professional help, participating in therapy sessions together, and collaborating with support networks to create a comprehensive and tailored approach to recovery.

Conclusion. The narratives woven through family testimonies serve as both a testament to the challenges families face when dealing with hikikomori and a source of inspiration for those navigating similar paths. By examining these real-life stories, we gain a deeper appreciation for the resilience of families, the efficacy of diverse coping mechanisms, and the transformative impact of unconditional support. Family testimonies not only contribute to a collective understanding of hikikomori but also provide a roadmap for fostering familial environments that nurture recovery and reconnection.

Family Testimony. Navigating the Path to Reconnection. Our family's journey through the labyrinth of hikikomori unfolded unexpectedly but with a determination to find a way back to connection. As parents, we discovered our son, Mark, retreating into the confines of his room at the age of 19, gradually disconnecting from the outside world. Here, we share our family testimony, a testament to the challenges we faced and the strategies that paved the way for Mark's recovery.

Discovery and Initial Reactions. The revelation of Mark's withdrawal was met with a mix of disbelief, concern, and confusion. Initially, our attempts to understand were met with resistance, and communication became strained. Family testimonies often begin with the realization that hikikomori is a shared challenge, a collective journey that requires united efforts.

Seeking Professional Guidance. In our pursuit of a path forward, we turned to professional guidance. Family testimonies frequently underscore the importance of seeking assistance from mental health professionals who specialize in hikikomori. Therapy sessions became a space where we, as a family, could unpack the complexities of social withdrawal and develop a collective understanding.

Creating a Supportive Environment. Our family testimony highlights the significance of creating a supportive environment. We learned to balance the need for boundaries with providing a safety net of understanding. The process involved reshaping our home dynamics, fostering an atmosphere where Mark felt heard and supported without judgment. This shift was pivotal in creating an environment conducive to his healing.

Patience and Consistent Support. Patience emerged as a recurring theme in our family testimony. Overcoming hikikomori requires time, and the journey is marked by gradual progress. Consistent support, even in the face of setbacks, became a cornerstone of our approach. Family testimonies often emphasize the importance of unwavering encouragement as individuals navigate the challenges of reintegration.

Encouraging Social Reconnection. Our family testimony includes the gradual steps taken to encourage social reconnection. We recognized the value of small victories, whether it was a brief outing or a shared family activity. These moments of connection became building blocks, reinforcing the idea that reintegration is a step-by-step process.

Learning and Growing Together. Family testimonies capture the transformative power of shared learning and growth. As a family, we underwent an evolution in our understanding of hikikomori and its complexities. Our testimony reflects the importance of adapting and growing together, creating a resilient family unit capable of supporting Mark through his journey.

Conclusion. Our family testimony is a narrative of hope, resilience, and the transformative power of familial support. It is a testament to the challenges faced, the lessons learned, and the unwavering commitment to reconnection. In sharing our story, we hope to contribute to the collective understanding of hikikomori and offer inspiration to families navigating similar paths. Family testimonies, in their authenticity, become guiding lights, illuminating the way toward healing and reconnection.

CHAPTER 9
BEYOND STIGMA

Shaping Public Perception
In the realm of hikikomori, public perception plays a pivotal role in either perpetuating stigma or fostering understanding. It is necessary to do the imperative task of shaping public perception through targeted advocacy efforts and awareness campaigns, with a focus on dismantling the misconceptions surrounding social withdrawal.

Understanding the Stigma. Before advocating for change, it is essential to comprehend the existing stigma associated with hikikomori. Public perception often tends to be influenced by misconceptions, labeling individuals as reclusive or lazy without understanding the complex psychological, social, and cultural factors that contribute to social withdrawal. This section aims to dissect these stereotypes and lay the groundwork for a more informed and empathetic perspective.

Humanizing the Experience. A key strategy in reshaping public perception involves humanizing the experience of hikikomori. Advocacy initiatives often feature real-life stories, testimonials, and multimedia presentations that put a face to social withdrawal. By presenting the human side of hikikomori, these efforts seek to evoke empathy and dismantle stereotypes, illustrating that behind the label are individuals with unique struggles, aspirations, and the potential for recovery.

Educational Initiatives. Advocacy for shaping public perception is closely tied to educational initiatives. This involves disseminating accurate information about hikikomori through various channels, including schools, community centers, and online platforms. Educational campaigns aim to debunk myths, raise awareness about the factors contributing to social withdrawal, and emphasize the importance of fostering a supportive and non-judgmental societal environment.

Media Representation and Responsible Reporting. The media plays a significant role in influencing public perception. Advocacy efforts target media outlets to encourage responsible reporting on hikikomori. This includes promoting accurate portrayals, avoiding sensationalism, and refraining from reinforcing stereotypes. Collaboration between advocacy groups and media organizations becomes a crucial step in ensuring that the narratives surrounding hikikomori are balanced, respectful, and contribute to informed public discourse.

Community Dialogues and Workshops. Shaping public perception is not a one-way process but involves engaging communities in open dialogues. Advocacy groups organize workshops, seminars, and community discussions to provide platforms for individuals affected by hikikomori, their families, and mental health professionals to share insights. These dialogues aim to foster understanding, address concerns, and encourage community-driven initiatives to support those experiencing social withdrawal.

Empowering Advocates. Central to reshaping public perception is empowering advocates who champion the cause. This involves providing training and resources for individuals with lived experiences, mental health professionals, and community leaders to become effective advocates. The collective voice of advocates serves as a powerful catalyst for change, challenging stigma, and driving the narrative towards a more compassionate understanding of hikikomori.

Conclusion. Shaping public perception is a dynamic and multifaceted endeavor that requires collaborative efforts from advocacy groups, individuals with lived experiences, and the broader community. By challenging stigma, humanizing the experience, promoting responsible media representation, conducting educational initiatives, and fostering community dialogues, this book aims to pave the way for a paradigm shift in how hikikomori is perceived. In doing so, the goal is to create a more inclusive, empathetic, and supportive societal response to social withdrawal.

Anti-Stigma Campaigns

Within the discourse of hikikomori, dismantling societal stigmas is a crucial step toward fostering empathy and understanding. This section explores the realm of anti-stigma campaigns, illuminating the strategies employed to reshape public perception and promote a more compassionate narrative surrounding social withdrawal.

Understanding Stigmas Associated with Hikikomori. Before delving into anti-stigma campaigns, it is essential to dissect the prevalent misconceptions and stereotypes attached to hikikomori. Public perceptions often frame social withdrawal as a result of personal choice or laziness, perpetuating stigmatizing beliefs that hinder empathy and hinder the development of effective support systems.

Objectives of Anti-Stigma Campaigns. Anti-stigma campaigns within the context of hikikomori are designed with specific objectives in mind. These campaigns seek to educate the public about the complexities of social withdrawal, challenge stereotypes, and highlight the multifaceted factors contributing to hikikomori. The overarching goal is to humanize the experience, replacing judgment with understanding.

Educational Initiatives. Central to anti-stigma campaigns is the implementation of educational initiatives. These may take the form of informational campaigns in schools, workplaces, and communities, providing accurate and nuanced portrayals of hikikomori. By disseminating knowledge about the psychological, social, and cultural dimensions of social withdrawal, these initiatives aim to dismantle preconceived notions.

Media Advocacy and Public Discourse. Harnessing the power of media advocacy, anti-stigma campaigns strategically engage with various media channels to reshape public discourse. This involves featuring authentic narratives, success stories, and expert perspectives in mainstream media, challenging sensationalism and fostering a more balanced representation of hikikomori. Media advocacy plays a pivotal role in influencing public opinion and dispelling myths.

Collaboration with Influencers and Advocates. Anti-stigma campaigns often leverage the reach and influence of social media influencers, celebrities, and advocates who align with the cause. These collaborations amplify the campaign's message, reaching diverse audiences and breaking through echo chambers. Personal testimonials from influencers can humanize the hikikomori experience, contributing to a more empathetic public discourse.

Community Engagement Events. Bringing the conversation about hikikomori directly to communities, anti-stigma campaigns organize events, workshops, and forums for open dialogue. These community engagement initiatives aim to create safe spaces for discussions, dispel misconceptions, and encourage individuals to share their experiences. Direct interaction fosters empathy and promotes a culture of acceptance.

Measuring Impact and Adjusting Strategies. The effectiveness of anti-stigma campaigns is assessed through ongoing evaluation and feedback mechanisms. Metrics such as shifts in public perception, increased awareness, and changes in policy attitudes are essential indicators. Campaigns are flexible, with strategies adjusted based on the evolving landscape to ensure sustained impact.

Conclusion. Anti-stigma campaigns stand as catalysts for societal change in the realm of hikikomori. By dismantling stereotypes, fostering understanding, and humanizing the experiences of those facing social withdrawal, these campaigns pave the way for a more inclusive and supportive societal response. The journey toward eradicating stigmas is ongoing, requiring collaborative efforts to create a culture where individuals experiencing hikikomori are met with empathy, dignity, and the support they deserve.

Advocacy Success Stories

In the pursuit of destigmatizing hikikomori and fostering a compassionate societal response, this section delves into advocacy success stories that showcase the transformative impact of initiatives aimed at reshaping public perception. These narratives highlight the pivotal role advocacy plays in building awareness, challenging stereotypes, and paving the way for empathetic understanding.

Shaping Public Perception. Advocacy success stories often commence with concerted efforts to shape public perception. Through targeted campaigns, individuals and organizations work towards dispelling myths surrounding hikikomori, replacing stigma with accurate information. These campaigns employ various mediums, such as social media, community events, and educational programs, to reach diverse audiences and challenge preconceived notions.

Anti-Stigma Campaigns. Anti-stigma campaigns emerge as powerful tools in the advocacy arsenal. Success stories within this realm detail strategic campaigns designed to confront stereotypes, reduce discrimination, and encourage open conversations about hikikomori. Personal testimonies, expert insights, and visual storytelling become integral components in humanizing the experience of social withdrawal and debunking misconceptions.

Community Engagement. Advocacy success stories frequently highlight the impact of community engagement initiatives. By fostering collaboration with local communities, advocates create spaces for dialogue, understanding, and support. Community forums, workshops, and support groups become platforms for individuals affected by hikikomori to share their experiences, reducing isolation and building connections within the community.

Advocacy in Educational Settings. Success stories within educational settings showcase the effectiveness of advocacy in influencing school environments and policies. Advocates work towards integrating hikikomori awareness into educational curricula, training educators to recognize warning signs, and implementing support systems for students at risk. By embedding awareness within educational institutions, advocates contribute to early intervention and prevention strategies.

Media Representation. Advocacy success stories within media representation underscore the importance of accurate portrayals in the press and entertainment industry. Collaborations with journalists, filmmakers, and content creators aim to depict hikikomori in a nuanced and empathetic light. Successes in this realm contribute to dismantling sensationalized narratives and fostering a more informed public discourse.

Policy Advocacy. In the realm of hikikomori advocacy, success stories in policy advocacy demonstrate the capacity to influence systemic change. Advocates work towards the development and implementation of policies that address the needs of individuals experiencing social withdrawal. These policy changes may encompass mental health support, educational reforms, and community integration initiatives.

Impact Assessment and Continuous Improvement. Advocacy success stories often include strategies for assessing impact and refining approaches. Advocates measure the effectiveness of campaigns, educational initiatives, and policy changes, using feedback loops to continually improve their methods. This iterative process ensures that advocacy efforts remain responsive to evolving societal needs and challenges.

Conclusion. Advocacy success stories within the hikikomori landscape showcase the potential for transformative change in societal attitudes. By challenging stigma, fostering awareness, and actively engaging communities, advocates contribute to creating a more empathetic and supportive environment for individuals facing social withdrawal. These success stories inspire continued efforts in the pursuit of a society that embraces diversity, understanding, and resilience in the face of hikikomori.

CHAPTER 10
PATHWAYS TO RECOVERY
AND FUTURE DIRECTIONS

Recovery Journeys of Hikikomori Individuals

As we reflect on the intricate journey of hikiko-mori, it is essential to delve into the inspiring narratives of individuals who have successfully navigated the challenging terrain of social withdrawal and emerged on the other side of recovery. This section, dedicated to the recovery journeys of hikikomori individuals, serves as a testament to resilience, transformation, and the diverse pathways toward reconnection.

These recovery journeys are not mere anecdotes; they represent triumphs over isolation, setbacks, and the complex web of factors contributing to hikikomori. Through these narratives, a common thread emerges — the power of human resilience and the potential for change, even in the face of seemingly insurmountable challenges.

Each recovery journey is as unique as the individuals themselves, reflecting the diversity of experiences within the realm of hikikomori. Some found solace and support through online communities, forging connections that became lifelines during moments of profound isolation. Others embarked on a gradual process of reintegration, taking small steps toward real-world interactions and reclaiming spaces outside the confines of their rooms.

Family support features prominently in many of these recovery journeys. The narratives highlight the crucial role of understanding, patience, and unwavering familial support in creating a foundation for healing. Family members, often transformed by the experience, become allies and advocates, contributing to the collective effort to break down the walls of hikikomori.

Educational reintegration is a recurring theme, underscoring the importance of flexible and personalized approaches to learning. Success stories within the realm of education illuminate innovative models that accommodate the needs of hikikomori individuals, allowing them to pursue academic goals while navigating the challenges of social reintegration.

Community involvement becomes a pivotal chapter in these recovery journeys. Local initiatives, support networks, and community engagement serve as catalysts for change. The narratives highlight the transformative impact of collective efforts in creating inclusive environments that foster acceptance and understanding.

Advocacy, too, plays a role in these recovery stories. Individuals who have reclaimed their lives from the clutches of hikikomori often become advocates, sharing their experiences to shape public perception and contribute to anti-stigma initiatives. Their voices amplify the call for empathy, awareness, and systemic changes in addressing social withdrawal.

In essence, the recovery journeys of hikikomori individuals are narratives of hope, resilience, and the enduring capacity for change. As we immerse ourselves in these stories, we gain not only a profound understanding of the challenges inherent in hikikomori but also insights into the diverse pathways that lead to recovery. These narratives inspire a collective call to action — a commitment to fostering environments that nurture reconnection, understanding, and a shared journey toward a future where hikikomori is met with empathy, support, and the belief in the transformative power of human connection.

Recovery Journey 1. Rediscovering Connection Through Online Support. Meet Alex, a 25-year-old who, after years of social withdrawal, found solace and support through online communities. Alex's journey began by connecting with others facing hikikomori through dedicated forums and chat groups. These virtual spaces provided a sense of belonging and understanding, enabling Alex to share experiences, fears, and hopes with individuals who could relate. Over time, these online connections evolved into genuine friendships, propelling Alex toward a journey of gradual reintegration into offline social interactions.

Recovery Journey 2. Family Support and Gradual Reintegration. Sophie, a 22-year-old, embarked on a recovery journey shaped by the unwavering support of her family. Recognizing the need for a patient and understanding approach, Sophie's family created a home environment that fostered open communication and empathy. Together, they worked on setting achievable goals for Sophie's reintegration, starting with small outings and gradually expanding to more extensive social interactions. Sophie's journey reflects the transformative impact of familial understanding and collaborative efforts in navigating the complexities of hikikomori.

Recovery Journey 3. Educational Reintegration and Personal Growth. Mark, a 20-year-old, found his path to recovery through innovative educational models. Enrolling in a flexible online education program allowed Mark to pursue academic interests at his own pace, free from the pressures of traditional schooling. This personalized approach not only facilitated Mark's educational reintegration but also became a catalyst for personal growth. Through the support of educators and mentors, Mark discovered a renewed sense of purpose, contributing to his holistic recovery from social withdrawal.

Recovery Journey 4. Community Engagement and Advocacy. Emma, a 28-year-old, discovered the transformative power of community engagement and advocacy in her recovery from hikikomori. Inspired by her own journey, Emma became actively involved in local initiatives aimed at supporting individuals facing social withdrawal. Through community outreach programs and support networks, Emma found a sense of purpose in helping others navigate their challenges. Emma's recovery journey extends beyond personal triumph to advocacy, contributing to the broader movement to destigmatize hikikomori and promote understanding within society.

These examples illustrate the diverse pathways individuals may take on their journey to recovery from hikikomori. While each story is unique, they share common themes of support, understanding, and the gradual process of reclaiming connection with the world. These recovery journeys underscore the importance of tailored approaches that consider the individual's needs, strengths, and the broader support systems available.

Research Gaps and Future Avenues

As we navigate the complex landscape of hikikomori recovery, it is imperative to identify existing research gaps and chart future avenues that can contribute to a more comprehensive understanding of social withdrawal. It is necessary to highlight areas where knowledge is still nascent and proposing directions for future exploration.

Research Gaps

Longitudinal Studies on Recovery Trajectories. Current research often provides snapshots of hikikomori individuals at specific points in their recovery journeys. Longitudinal studies tracking individuals over extended periods are needed to capture the dynamic nature of recovery trajectories. Understanding the factors influencing relapses and sustained recovery can inform more targeted interventions.

Cultural Variances in Recovery Strategies. While existing research acknowledges cultural influences on the manifestation of hikikomori, there is a gap in understanding how cultural contexts shape recovery strategies. Comparative studies across different cultures can provide insights into culturally sensitive approaches to recovery and reintegration.

The Role of Technology in Recovery. While technology is implicated in the onset of hikikomori, its role in the recovery process remains understudied. Exploring how digital platforms, online communities, and technological interventions contribute to or hinder recovery can offer nuanced insights into leveraging technology as a tool for support.

Intersectionality and Recovery. Research often examines hikikomori as a standalone phenomenon, with limited exploration of how intersecting factors such as gender, socioeconomic status, and mental health conditions impact recovery. Future studies should adopt an intersectional lens to uncover the unique challenges and strengths that different demographic groups bring to the recovery process.

Future Avenues
Development of Tailored Intervention Programs. Future research should focus on developing and evaluating intervention programs tailored to the diverse needs of hikikomori individuals. This includes considering variations in age, cultural background, and the presence of co-occurring conditions. Tailored interventions can enhance the efficacy of recovery efforts.

Exploration of Peer Support Dynamics. Peer support networks play a crucial role in recovery, yet the dynamics of these networks are not fully understood. Research should explore how peer support evolves over time, the impact of online communities, and the factors that contribute to the success of peer-led initiatives in promoting reconnection.

Integration of Technology-Assisted Therapies. Investigating the integration of technology-assisted therapies, such as virtual reality interventions and telehealth services, can open new avenues for supporting hikikomori individuals. Understanding the benefits and challenges of these technological approaches can inform the development of innovative and accessible recovery tools.

Community-Based Participatory Research. Engaging hikikomori individuals, their families, and communities in the research process can enhance the relevance and applicability of findings. Community-based participatory research approaches can empower stakeholders to actively contribute to the identification of recovery strategies and the development of supportive interventions.

By addressing these research gaps and exploring future avenues, the field of hikikomori research can evolve to provide more nuanced, culturally sensitive, and effective approaches to support individuals on their journey to recovery and reconnection. This ongoing exploration is crucial for developing a holistic understanding of hikikomori and advancing evidence-based practices for intervention and support.

Concluding Thoughts and Recommendations
As we conclude this exploration into the multifaceted realm of hikikomori, it is crucial to reflect on the insights gained and chart a course toward future directions. The recovery journeys, diverse strategies, and collective efforts showcased throughout this discourse provide a foundation for understanding and addressing social withdrawal. In this concluding section, we offer thoughts and recommendations that extend beyond the individual narratives, envisioning a future where hikikomori is met with empathy, support, and comprehensive interventions.

Understanding the Nuances of Hikikomori. A fundamental takeaway from this exploration is the need for a nuanced understanding of hikikomori. Recognizing the diversity of experiences, triggers, and recovery paths is essential. By acknowledging the intricate interplay of psychosocial, familial, and societal factors, we can develop interventions that are tailored, empathetic, and effective.

Fostering Collaborative Approaches. The recovery journeys presented highlight the transformative power of collaboration. Be it through online support communities, familial understanding, educational institutions, or advocacy networks, the collective efforts of individuals, families, communities, and professionals play a pivotal role. Fostering a collaborative approach that integrates diverse perspectives and expertise is crucial for creating a supportive ecosystem for hikikomori individuals.

Prioritizing Mental Health Support. Central to the recovery narratives is the significance of mental health support. As we move forward, there is a pressing need to prioritize mental health resources, destigmatize seeking help, and integrate mental health education into various facets of society. This proactive approach can contribute to early intervention, reducing the severity and duration of social withdrawal.

Tailoring Educational Systems. Educational reintegration emerges as a key theme in many recovery journeys. This calls for a reevaluation of traditional educational systems to accommodate the diverse needs of hikikomori individuals. Flexible models, personalized learning approaches, and comprehensive mental health support within educational settings can pave the way for successful academic reintegration.

Promoting Community Involvement and Awareness. Community engagement is a driving force in many recovery stories. Encouraging local initiatives, support networks, and awareness campaigns can create environments that foster understanding and acceptance. By actively involving communities, we contribute to the creation of inclusive spaces that support individuals in their journey toward reconnection.

Advancing Research and Advocacy. The narratives underscore the importance of ongoing research and advocacy. Investing in studies that delve into the root causes, effective interventions, and long-term outcomes of hikikomori is crucial. Simultaneously, advocacy efforts should strive to destigmatize social withdrawal, shape public perception, and influence policy changes that promote holistic support systems.

Encouraging Open Dialogues. This exploration reveals the transformative power of open dialogues surrounding hikikomori. Promoting conversations at the individual, familial, community, and societal levels can break down barriers and challenge misconceptions. Open dialogues contribute to a culture of understanding, compassion, and shared responsibility in addressing the complexities of social withdrawal.

In conclusion, the recovery journeys of hikikomori individuals illuminate a path forward—one that prioritizes empathy, collaboration, and proactive intervention. By embracing these principles, we can collectively work toward a future where hikikomori is not met with judgment but rather with a supportive and informed response. The narratives shared in this discourse serve as beacons of hope, urging us to envision a society where every individual, regardless of their journey, has the opportunity for healing, reconnection, and a meaningful future.

SIMPLE SHORT BOOKS

The simple short books every reader desires.

Printed in Great Britain
by Amazon